AN ENDURING WITNESS

with Riley K. Smith

Pakistan: An Enduring Witness

VOM Books
P.O. Box 443
Bartlesville, OK 74005-0443

Previously published by Living Sacrifice Books, an imprint of The Voice of the Martyrs.

ISBN 978-0-88264-034-1

Edited by Lynn Copeland

Cover design by Lookout Design

Cover creation, page design, and layout by Genesis Group

Printed in the United States of America

Reprinted April 2013

"But recall the former days in which . . . you endured a great struggle with sufferings: partly while you were made a spectacle both by reproaches and tribulations, and partly while you became companions of those who were so treated; for you had compassion on me in my chains, and joyfully accepted the plundering of your goods, knowing that you have a better and an enduring possession for yourselves in heaven. Therefore do not cast away your confidence, which has great reward.

"For you have need of endurance, so that after you have done the will of God, you may receive the promise."

—THE WRITER OF HEBREWS (10:32–36)

"The Christians persecuted in one village flee to another, and are often without any certain dwelling place: being reviled, they bless; being persecuted, they meekly submit; defamed, they entreat. They suffer hunger, thirst, nakedness..., and are counted as the filth of the world—the off-scouring of all things. By the fire of the persecutions... come forth the gold and silver, tried and purified for the Master's building.

"Enemies beholding the faith and patience of the suffering disciples, are converted, and give glory to God; and in the midst of these scenes the Lord is building up a glorious Church, as enduring and indestructible as the eternal Rock upon which it rests."

—ANDREW GORDON, *Our India Mission*, speaking of Christian converts in northwestern India (present-day Pakistan)

CONTENTS

ACKNOWLEDGMENTS

There are several people who were so helpful in the writing, editing, and production of this book. First, thank you, Dory P., for the research materials you provided regarding your article for *The Voice of the Martyrs* newsletter. Your love for Pakistan and those who suffer for Christ's name are evident in your work. I appreciate those who reviewed the first draft and answered several questions related to the situation in Pakistan, yet must remain nameless. The risks you take to serve our persecuted family do not go unnoticed, and I pray for you and your families as you do the Lord's work. I would also like to thank David Hepworth. David, thank you for your persistence in tracking down permissions on a few of the photos, which will make several people and events in this book seem more real to the reader. Thank you, Lynn Copeland, for your edits and questions that further enhance the book's message. And thank you, Lynn Timm, for diligently coordinating and working behind the scenes to get this book in print.

Finally, my deepest thanks for the enduring witness of Christians throughout Pakistan's history to today who with the Psalmist cry out, "The Lord is for me; I will not fear; what can man do to me?" (Psalm 118:6, NASB). For those who read this book, thank you for taking the time to understand the historical and political context of Christian persecution in Pakistan. In most restricted nations, persecution didn't happen overnight with the change of a political leader or a foreign invasion. As you will read on the following pages, even laws that were created with good intentions can go wrong when interpreted by those with ulterior motives. May the words in this book inspire you to become involved in helping our persecuted family in Pakistan!

RILEY K. SMITH

INTRODUCTION:
A MARTYR IN A NEW NATION

She was born Qamar Zia. As one of seven children in a Muslim family, Qamar was introduced to the Bible when her parents had to transfer her from a government school to a Christian one. One teacher there was different, having a faith that inspired Qamar.

Qamar began studying the Bible. When she reached Isaiah 53, she had made up her mind. Perhaps it was the prophet's depiction of Jesus bearing our griefs and carrying our sorrows or how He was wounded for our transgressions. She placed her trust in Jesus Christ. Furious about her newfound faith, her parents removed her from the school.

When India gained its independence from Britain in 1947, Qamar's family decided to immigrate with tens of thousands of other Muslims to the newly formed country that broke from India: Pakistan. Her family chose to settle in Karachi, Pakistan. Little is known how Qamar managed to contact a missionary named Marian, but she did. She was determined to know more about following Jesus.

Having requested a Bible, Qamar grew in her faith as she read the words secretly, knowing it would make her parents angry if they found out.

But soon, her faith would lead her to make a decision that would force her to leave her family for good.

Her parents had arranged for her to marry a Muslim man. Refusing to marry a Muslim, she ran away and stayed with Marian. Marian found her a job, and Qamar changed her name to Esther John. (A name change is customary when a person converts to a different religion in Pakistan.) However, despite her move, her family continued to pressure her to marry the man they had arranged for her.

Esther couldn't take the pressure any longer. One day she boarded a train north for Sahiwal, Punjab province, several hundred miles away.

With a new name and new surroundings, Esther worked in a mission hospital and eventually enrolled in a school to become a teacher. All the while, she stayed in touch with her family, even visiting them during holidays.

Though they sometimes welcomed her home

Esther John

and did not pressure her to return to Islam, at other times her family pressured her to return home to them in Karachi for good.

After completing her studies, Esther moved another thirty miles away to Chichawatni, where she lived with American missionaries. She rode her bicycle from village to village, sharing the gospel, teaching women how to read, and helping them work the fields. But her ministry soon came to a sudden end.

In 1959, Esther sent her family a letter, agreeing to visit them after Christmas but only on two conditions: that they not push her into marrying a Muslim and that they allow her to remain a Christian. Her family never replied.

On the morning of February 2, 1960, Esther was found murdered in her bed, her skull crushed. No investigation was conducted to discover who killed Esther. Some believe one of her brothers had murdered her.

The first recorded martyrdom in the new nation called Pakistan, Esther's story had made such an impact that Westminster Abbey had a statue created in honor of her witness. It is hard to say how many others were martyred for their Christian witness besides Esther. Many have likely died without an official record; only the Lord knows with their details recorded and awaiting the Day of Judgment. No one knows. But Esther's story represents what many Christians in Pakistan face today: rejection and coercion by the Muslim majority.

Despite it being legal in Pakistan for Muslims to change their religion, non-Muslims face life with few to no opportunities. When Britain released its hold on India and Pakistan became its own country, Christians had a decision to make: become citizens in India's Hindu-dominated culture, or become citizens in Pakistan's Muslim-dominated society.

The following pages share the story of such challenges for Christians in Pakistan, reaching as far back as the early centuries after the apostles divided up the regions to evangelize the known world, to today. By no means intended as a comprehensive history, this book shares what believers have faced as they struggled to survive under changing dictators when a part of India.

You will learn about the overcoming courage of one man who pursued Western missionaries, insisting they share the good news of the gospel with him. For this, he endured rejection and persecution but eventually his entire caste was reached within decades. You will read Pakistan's story of its conspicuous transition from a nation intended for all peoples and religions, to a nation that ensured the domination of Islam. But the greatest test confronting the church in Pakistan has come through the legalization of a law rooted in British Colonial history that has been used to silence the

Christians' gospel witness and to keep them as inferior, second-class citizens.

Despite the blatant injustices and wrongs committed against Christians in today's Pakistan, they have an enduring witness, determined to stay true to Christ in a Muslim-dominated society. As you read their stories, may they inspire you to have a witness for Christ that endures!

DIGGING FOR ROOTS: CHRISTIANITY'S BEGINNINGS IN PAKISTAN

They are searching for identity, legitimacy, and belonging in their new nation. As today's Pakistani Christians struggle to find their place in a Muslim society and refute accusations that they merely follow a Western religion, many are on a quest for evidence to prove Christianity's presence prior to Islam's arrival in the eighth century. And much has been found. Crosses, coins, kings, and claims have uncovered clues to their roots. However, these objects and legends have neither confirmed nor contested Christianity's official arrival in Pakistan, a country with a history rooted in India's prior to its birth in 1947.

Some say the apostle Thomas brought the gospel to present-day Pakistan. The apocryphal tale *The Acts of Thomas* tells the story of a reluctant Thomas who finally concedes to go to India. King Gondolphares allegedly reigned over parts of Persia and present-day Pakistan. Hiring Thomas to build a palace for him, the king supposedly discovers that Thomas had used his money for the poor—not his palace—and throws Thomas in prison. Though the king orders Thomas' execution, the king's brother dies and appears to the sovereign in a dream, conveying a message in favor of the apostle. Thomas is released and continues evangelizing but is once again imprisoned, this time by King Misdaeus, who has the apostle put to death.

Coins have been unearthed supporting the existence of King Gondolphares, making it likely that *The Acts of*

© Classical Numismatic Group, Inc., www.cngcoins.com

Unearthed coins supporting the existence of King Gondolphares

Thomas does contain some historical accuracy, and that Thomas therefore could have brought the gospel to Pakistan.

Local legends also assert Thomas's presence in parts of present-day Pakistan. Residents of Garthoma in the district of Islamabad claim that a disaster hit northern Punjab and their village was the only one unharmed. Thinking the apostle's visit had something to do with averting certain destruction, they named the village after him.

Then in 1935, archaeologists dug up a cross allegedly dating back to the second century. Decades later, the Anglican Church of Lahore adopted the cross as its church's symbol viewing it as evidence of Christianity's long-standing presence in Muslim-dominated Pakistan. But questions still linger over the cross's true age. An additional claim to Christian history has been made by the

Taxila historical society, which believes that one of the magi who visited Baby Jesus—Melchior—was a Pakistani scholar from the ancient university in Taxila.

Despite the conjecture, we do know for certain that Christianity had a presence in Pakistan well before the arrival of Islam in the seventh century. However, the question is precisely *when*. If not the apostle Thomas, some say the first Christian presence was due to Christians fleeing the Persian shah's persecution in the fourth century.

What we also know is that Christianity's presence waned in Pakistan during the Middle Ages. By the end of the eleventh century, Christian communities in Baluchistan, Punjab, and Sind were said to be virtually nonexistent. Not until

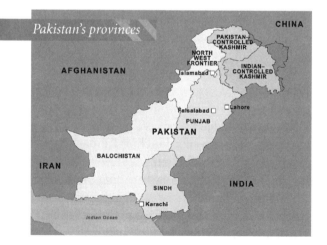

Pakistan's provinces

the arrival of the Europeans around the fifteenth and sixteenth centuries did Christianity once again take root. Catholics arrived first and then Protestants. And in southern India, pockets of Christians who professed direct lineage to the apostle Thomas' first converts were discovered.

In time the gospel message spread but not without opposition and hostility. At times, Western colonists ambitious to amass riches on the subcontinent would anger the local *rajahs* (Indian rulers or princes) and even Muslim leaders to the north. Therefore, anything Western, including missionaries whose gaze was not fixed on earthly riches, would be caught in their ire. Those who dared to turn from Hinduism or Islam faced rejection and beatings from family and officials. And it is a trend that would continue for centuries for Christians in this part of India that would one day be called Pakistan.

CONQUEST AND COERCION:
THE ARRIVAL OF ISLAM

It was more than political. It was a religious duty, one which required them to convert the infidels —the idol-worshiping Hindus—to Islam in their quest to subject the entire world to Allah.

Around A.D. 711, Arab invaders led by General Muhammad bin Qasim conquered Sind in northwestern India. Since then, Islam has held fast its grip on this area in present-day Pakistan —and has never let go.

Taking their divine commission seriously, bin Qasim and his men forcibly circumcised the high-caste Hindus, called Brahmans, in Debul. When the Hindus opposed the painful Islamic conversion requirement for men, bin Qasim ordered that all males age seventeen and older be put to death.

The conquered now had a choice to make: One, become a part of the *dhimma*, a treaty agreement where non-Muslims pay a high tax called a *jizya* in exchange for "peace"; two, convert to Islam to avoid the financially debilitating tax; or three, refuse either and die.

In the centuries that followed, Islam did not take root throughout the rest of the subcontinent. Of the countries Islam had already conquered, the religion would never remain and overcome the people and penetrate the political institution; that is, not in southern India. Northwestern India, which would become Pakistan, is another story altogether.

It wasn't until A.D. 1001 that northern India faced another major onslaught from Islamic invaders. This time, the attackers were not Arab. They were Turkish, led by Mahmud of Gazni. From the mountains of Afghanistan, Mahmud led his men into northwestern India where they plundered and overpowered the polytheistic peoples. Despite about a dozen raids over twenty-five years, his only lasting colony was Lahore—a city in present-day Pakistan—which would develop into an Islamic cultural and educational center.

Mahmud was by no means the last of the Muslim conquerors to invade this vulnerable region of India. In 1202, Islam's influence extended to Bengal under Bakhtyar Khalji.

The Turkish sultanates held sway in parts of India until its domain was slowly disrupted by the Mughals (or Mongols, those who followed Genghis Khan). First it was Tamerlane's invasion in the fourteenth century that all but annihilated the church of the East, leaving a remnant of survivors in southern India and Kurdistan. Then in the next few hundred years, the Turks' power was finally usurped with Babur's invasion in 1525. The following year Babur established the Mughal Empire in northern India. And during the reign of Akbar in 1556 until Aurangzib in 1707, Islam reached its pinnacle on the subcontinent.

Throughout Islam's quest to control the sub-continent, its conquerors used extreme measures to coerce the people to follow Islam. In the four-teenth century, Firuz Shah (1351–1388) ordered a Brahman to be burned to death after refusing to convert to Islam. The Brahman was accused of worshiping Hindu idols in his home and alleged-ly leading Muslim women away from their faith. Even in the mid-eighteenth century, under orders of Ahmad Shah Abdali, ninety thousand men and women were taken as prisoners and forced to con-vert to Islam. Then as late as 1921, in what was called the Moplah Rebellion, Muslims bent on restoring the old Turkish caliphate (the territory under a caliph, or person in authority) took up arms and killed those who refused to convert.

Since its arrival in the early eighth century, Islam would function only as a corresponding culture to Hinduism, never fully subjecting the entire country to its rituals and religion as it had in other conquered lands. According to one source, by the end of the 1700s, Islam became less coer-cive. Perhaps with India a British colony, its strong military arm forced the fiery Islamic commanders and their followers to acclimate and acquiesce.

With these opposing religious cultures coex-isting and Islam holding fast in the northwest, a tension developed that would one day lead to

India's and Pakistan's partition in 1947. However, during Islam's occupation in areas, missionaries would arrive from the West, and the church would experience glimmers of hope that perhaps a Muslim Mughal emperor would embrace Christianity. But first, Christians in India's northwest would be effected by leaders bent on Islamic dominance, such as Tipu Sultan in 1799.

STORY FROM HISTORY:
THE BRUTALITY OF TIPU SULTAN

First it was the Arabs, then the Turks, and finally the Mughals. By the early fourteenth century, Muslim invaders had overrun the northern section of India all the way south to the Vindhya Mountains. In fact, some believe Christianity was all but extinct, purged from certain areas, one of which would later be known as Pakistan.

With Islam's sword conquering portions of southern India, one Muslim ruler stood out among the others. His commitment to converting the "infidels" became his war cry, unleashing a brutality that left his victims bloodied and maimed and with little choice but to convert to his religion or succumb to his sword. His name was Tipu Sultan. And though his violent acts occurred in the south, some say they stand as proof of Christianity's decline in northern and central India under Islamic domination.

His rage began in 1784, in retaliation for a group of Catholics who allied with the British in a previous war. Tipu and his men took the inhabitants of Canara by surprise, forcing their mass exodus to Mysore. An estimated forty thousand people were taken captive, ordered to walk the long journey. Many died along the way from hunger and disease, and those who refused to cooperate with the soldiers were tortured, their noses and ears cut off. Tipu ordered his men to destroy the churches and let his soldiers take whatever the Christians had left behind.

In 1799, upon Tipu's death, their captivity came to an end. When the surviving Christians returned, they discovered that their property had been taken from them. Still, they set down roots and rebuilt their churches.

The captivity of Canara wasn't Tipu's only act of aggression, and Christians weren't his only victims. In a letter dated December 14, 1788, Tipu wrote to his army chief in Calicut (not to be confused with Calcutta): "I am sending two of my followers with Mir Hussain Ali. With their assistance, you should capture and kill all Hindus. Those below the age of 20 may be kept in prison and 5,000 from the rest should be killed by hanging... These are my orders." Months earlier, he gave further proof of his zeal for Islamic conversion when he wrote, "Over 12,000 Hindus were 'honored with Islam.'"

Not even women and children were spared.

In 1789, Tipu lashed out at the residents of Calicut and those in a nearby district. Again, it was in retaliation for their assisting a previous ruler. He sent thirty thousand men ahead of him, with orders to butcher anyone who got in their way. Riding on an elephant with another thirty thousand men behind him, Tipu set out to teach the people a lesson in loyalty. He hanged men as well as women. He tied up mothers and hanged their children. On his orders, several Christians and Hindus were stripped naked and tied to the feet of his elephant and dragged until they lost their limbs.

Churches and Hindu temples were destroyed. Any Christians who survived were forced to marry Muslim spouses. Several reports on this incident

Tipu Sultan

note that he forcibly circumcised many, perhaps even tens of thousands. Some managed to escape and tell of the atrocities committed against them.

But the damage was done. During his fifteen-year reign, an inestimable number of Christians were either killed or forced to convert to Islam under penalty of death. These men and women —even children—watched as blood was shed and bodies dismembered.

The church would soon be strengthened and rebuilt. Missionaries would arrive from the West, and their work would equip those left behind.

ONE CONVERT, ONE REQUEST, ONE MASS MOVEMENT: THE WORK OF MISSIONARIES

Foreign missionaries had a problem. As many Hindus embraced Christianity, the converts were hated for betraying the faith they were born into. Most faced the same fate: Their families rejected them. They were refused food. Their lives were threatened. They were locked in dark rooms. Some were poisoned or beaten. Their villages denied them access to water wells. They lost their jobs. Missionaries came to believe that the village environment was so wrought with temptations that it was almost impossible for converts to stay true to their newfound faith in Christ.

The nineteenth-century missionaries tried to help by giving material assistance directly to the new Christians. But this soon proved to create a dependency. Then the missionaries tried employing converts in their homes or at their mission compound. This, too, was far from ideal. Other experiments were tried. New converts even congregated together, creating their own communities.

Eventually, many new converts were invited to live on the missionary compound where they received training and physical safety to preserve their faith. This, too, would have long-term negative consequences, causing Christianity in present-day Pakistan to be viewed as a religion from the West, since the compound was led by Westerners. In addition, it prevented these new converts from living out their newfound faith in front of their people.

But one day the missionaries' approach to helping the persecuted converts would be challenged when a small, lame man by the name of Ditt stood on the doorstep of the mission compound in the Sialkot district and asked to be baptized.

Ditt was a Chuhra, one of the lowest castes in northwestern India (what is now northern Pakistan). Society despised the Chuhras, and used the label as a derogatory term. The Chuhras worked the most menial of tasks that were considered "unclean" by Hindus and Muslims alike. Considered to be among the "untouchables" of the Hindu caste system,[1] the Chuhras would remove the carcasses of animals from land, skin dead animals, and clean toilets. They often ate the food others had discarded and were viewed as drunks, shamelessly dependent on others, foolish, and lacking ambition. Unable to discern their genuine desire to know Christ and worried that working with such untouchables would offend other potential converts, missionaries were skeptical of

---

1 For more on the Hindu caste system, read *Restricted Nations: India.*

working with them. However, one Chuhra would change the missionaries' mind.

Having heard the gospel from a recent Hindu convert, Ditt couldn't resist this message of hope for a man in a very hopeless situation. Within a matter of decades, the conversion of this man Ditt would cause almost his entire caste to turn to Christ. However, it would not have happened without his unusual and strange request.

After Ditt had arrived at the Sialkot mission for baptism, one of the missionaries invited him to stay with them and receive more teaching in the faith. Ditt refused. Knowing what Ditt was going to face in his home village, the missionary was likely stunned by this small man's insistence on returning to share the good news of Jesus Christ. Up to that time, so many others had quickly accepted the invitation to stay that the missionaries believed it was neither possible nor wise for new converts to return to their village and remain faithful to Christ.

The missionary tried to convince Ditt to stay, yet he refused and returned home. In time Ditt would prove the missionaries wrong.

Three months after he visited the missionary compound, Ditt brought two new converts—his wife and daughter—for baptism. They, too, returned to the village with him.

His newfound faith was no secret. As a dealer in animal hides, he shared the gospel as he traveled from village to village. Many people placed their faith in Christ. But the more he shared, the more he was opposed.

Among Ditt's fiercest opponents were his own relatives. They would unite against him and hold "indignation meetings" where those in attendance would mock him, calling him a *Sahib* (a term applied to foreigners) or a *Be-imam* (meaning "one without religion"). His sister-in-law placed a curse on him, saying, "You have changed your religion without counseling with us. Our relationship is at the end. You will not eat, drink, or associate with us in any way. May your other leg break as well!"

Even so, Ditt remained unshaken and graciously replied, "Very well, my brethren; if it pleases you, you may oppose me and load me with reproaches and abuse; but your opposition will never induce me to deny Christ."

He continued sharing the gospel and taking his converts to the missionary compound for baptism. One family member placed his faith in Christ and even joined him in his gospel efforts.

About eighty years later, almost all the members of the Chuhra caste had become Christians, and it all began when one man refused the safety of the missionary compound and courageously evangelized despite the jeers and insults. His insistence on returning to live in his village challenged the foreign missionaries—as well as their national converts—that it was possible to stay true to Christ amid suffering and persecution for one's faith. In time history would refer to Ditt's and his caste's mass conversion as the Chuhra Movement.

Under the Mughals

Well before Ditt's conversion and subsequent baptism by Protestant missionaries, Catholic missionaries had already arrived in northwestern India (present-day Pakistan). Around 1600, Jesuits built a church in Lahore. Akbar, the Mughal[2] emperor at the time, was friendly toward the Catholic missionaries and even invited a few to his court to debate with other religious leaders.

Excited at the prospect of another Constantine should Akbar convert to Christianity, the Jesuits' hopes faded when Akbar announced his new religion, which was a conglomeration of several, including Christianity. It became clear that he had no intention of becoming a Christian.

Despite their failure at converting the Mughal emperor, one of the Jesuits was able to secure a written decree allowing public preaching and conversion. However, the Jesuits were not favored among all Mughal leaders.

Qulij Khan, a Sunni Muslim and the Viceroy of Lahore, was not so fond of the foreign men of

---

2 For more on the presence of Mughals in India and their effect on the church, read *Restricted Nations: India.*

God. One day he approached the Jesuits and asked, "How do you view Jesus Christ?"

"He is the Son of God," they replied.

Furious at their confident claim, the Viceroy threatened to cut off their heads, only to be refuted by the Jesuits' willingness to die.

Qulij then threatened their reputations by calling them names—vagabonds, seducers, cheaters—and ordered that they stay home and keep quiet about the gospel. The Jesuits responded that they would share about Christ not only at home, but also in the city center, in the streets, and in other public places. Finally, remembering their favor with the Mughal emperor and the decree that gave them the freedom to preach, the Viceroy had decided to say nothing else.

Soon, he devised another plan: Kidnap the wives and children of the new converts and force them to renounce their faith. The Jesuits were warned of the plan and the children were hidden. But the Viceroy's plan fell apart. On the very day the plan was to be carried out, the Viceroy's son came home from the battlefield, defeated. The Viceroy was so distraught at his son's loss that the kidnapping never occurred.

The Viceroy of Lahore was not the only source of the Christians' troubles. In succeeding Mughal leaders, their tolerance of Christians would wax and wane. Churches would be closed, and in some cases, Christians would flee to other areas because the pressure was so great.

One of the Mughal emperors more hostile toward Christians was Aurangzeb (reigning 1658–1707). In 1668, he began by ordering the destruction of Hindu temples and forbidding non-Muslims to display religious symbols in public. At first his decrees against Hindus didn't have much effect on the Christians in Lahore, but in Thatta (near Karachi) they would contribute to the Catholic missions' closure.

In 1669, Mughal officials confiscated a library belonging to the Carmelites, a Catholic religious order, who had been in Thatta since 1618, and interrogated them. They were accused of instructing Muslim children and sending them to Goa (along the southwestern coast) for baptism, causing a public scandal with their showy Christian celebrations, and possessing a copy of the Persian translation of *Contra Gentiles*.[3]

The priests were not publicly punished, but their position became less secure. In the end, Father Dionysius closed the mission. A few of his reasons included the amount of funds needed to repair and reconstruct the church in order to re-

---

3 Likely referring to Thomas Aquinas' *Summa Contra Gentiles*, a collection of writings that many believed to be a handbook for Christian missionaries in their work among Muslims. However, some debate the true purpose of the piece.

open it, but mostly, tragically, he had lost hope of seeing any new converts.

Apparently, the final end to the Jesuits' mission came not from the Muslim Mughals but from the West: Portugal. When Sebastian Joseph de Carvalho e Melo became dictator of Portugal, he set out to end the Jesuits' influence. Over the course of five years in the mid-eighteenth century, he suppressed the Jesuits in Portuguese territories. France and Spain did the same. But it was Sebastian who forced the papacy to bring the order to a close in 1773.

The Jesuits' end and the Carmelites' departure by no means brought an end to Christianity. It remained and spread with Protestant missionaries arriving in 1833. It was no easy road for the missionaries, but it was much harder for their converts, as previously mentioned.

As Christianity spread, so did Islam. And in time, Muslims would organize themselves into a league that would push for a country of their own.

STORY FROM HISTORY:
THE WITNESS OF PIPO (CIRCA 1860)

The native evangelist sat outside his tent, looking intently into the faces of the Meg people gathered outside their village of Jhandran. As members of a caste of weavers, they wanted to follow Jesus, but Muslim landowners were making it difficult for them. Since professing a faith in Christ, they refused to work on the Sabbath, angering their Muslim overlords.

Instead of enduring the hostility, they sought a compromise to appease their persecutors while following Christ. They proposed to the evangelist that they keep the rituals from their old religion, which included idol worship. In addition, they wanted to work on the Sabbath and view Jesus as an equal with their own religious teachers.

The evangelist's response was immediate and instinctive.

"No man," he responded, "can cross a river on two boats. You must forsake all for Christ, or you will not be counted worthy of Him."

The Megs understood: with Jesus, it was all or nothing. Would they be willing to endure the cost for following Christ, even despite their long search for a better religion?

More than two years ago, they had been duped by a visiting guru who promised to reveal God to them. After teaching the villagers for eighteen months, the guru's true beliefs finally became known: There is no heaven or hell. There is no one who requires an account of man. There is no one greater than man.

Shocked and angered, the villagers felt betrayed. The guru was really nothing more than an atheist.

One of the Megs, named Pipo, knew there was something more.

"There is, after all, One who is greater than man—One who gives life, gives us a spirit, and takes it again—and to Him must we give account," Pipo told the guru. "There is a Great Creator who made the earth and heavens."

After sending the guru away, Pipo and the remaining villagers continued their search for the one true God.

Months later, a new visitor arrived in Jhandran. Advanced in age and hardly able to read, Joahir Masih stopped at the sugar mill just outside the Megs' village. Many of the residents were preparing bundles of sugar cane for the mill while others boiled down the juice and shaped it into balls to sell at the market.

Seeing an opportunity, Joahir pulled out his New Testament and began reading from one of the Gospels. His timid voice immediately caught the attention of the Meg workers, who wondered if the man had come to announce some new government ordinance. But he didn't. The words he read intrigued the workers who were fascinated with the term "Son of God" that Joahir kept repeating in the text.

After he finished his reading from a chapter in the Gospels, Joahir looked out over the crowd.

"My brethren," he said, "you should repent, and you should believe on the Son of God, for the kingdom of heaven is at hand."

Suddenly, the clang of the sugar mill was silenced, and workers dropped the bunches of bound sugar cane from their hands. They murmured to each other, wondering if he was speaking of the truth they were seeking.

Word spread of Joahir's teaching and for three days and nights he taught the people, answering their questions, with barely any time to eat or sleep. Seeing their need for more teaching, Joahir took some of the Megs to a group of foreign missionaries who had lived nearby. The foreigners gave them copies of the Gospels, the Book of Acts, and *Pilgrim's Progress* to take back with them.

A week later, the native evangelist traveled with Joahir and others to Jhandran to visit the seeking Megs. While they were there, one of Pipo's relatives was married with three hundred guests in attendance. For three days they feasted and the evangelist preached.

Pipo was the first to profess his faith in Christ at the wedding celebration. After him, almost all of the twenty-five Meg families in Jhandran, as well as visitors from other villages, expressed a desire to follow Christ.

But their new faith did not go unnoticed or unopposed. An influential landowner named Diyala was not so pleased with the decision of the more than two dozen families. As an idol worshiper who led the Megs in rituals, he was angered at his loss of status within the village. He wasn't alone in his rage. The land surrounding Jhandran was owned by powerful Muslims who hated the gospel. And since the Megs worked for them, they were furious when their employees refused to work on the Sabbath.

Soon, the professed believers had another problem: they had already negotiated marriage partners for their children, some of whom were not Christians. Not only were the wedding ceremonies full of idolatrous rituals, but changing one's religion affected the marriage contract.

Not knowing what else to do, they attempted to compromise on a few of the Ten Commandments that were causing them trouble with the marriage arrangements and area landowners.

"No man can cross a river on two boats," responded the evangelist.

Pipo, Fakira, and a few others stepped forward from among the crowd.

"We are willing to give up everything for Jesus," they pledged.

The Megs were stunned by these words as they turned their attention to the men. This small handful would be the only ones willing to forsake all for Christ, as the remaining Meg "converts" returned to their idol-worshiping ways in order to maintain peace.

From that time on, Pipo, Fakira, and the others paid dearly for their decision. Muslims in the village persecuted the men, prohibiting them from drawing water from the village well. They beat them, hurting Pipo so terribly that it took him six months to recover. They had resolved to drive the faithful men from their village homes.

The Muslims weren't the only ones who harassed Pipo and Fakira. Those Megs who had rejected Christ were equally brutal, if not more so.

Village authorities ordered them to prepare a feast for the village and surrounding areas at their expense, return the Christian books and Gospels that the missionaries had given them, and stop communicating with the missionaries. If they refused to obey, they couldn't eat or drink with the others or draw from the village water well. Neither could anyone sell them food or conduct any sort of business with them.

Fakira and some of the converts held out for a year before finally conceding to the demands.

They paid a fine, returned the books, and cut off all communication with the missionaries.

Pipo didn't. He kept his New Testament. He could be beaten and kicked out of his home, but his love for Christ was so great that he could not turn his back on Him.

One night Pipo had managed to meet secretly with the evangelist who had pitched his tent outside the village. Discouraged and depressed, Pipo felt all alone in his Christian journey.

"Can I follow Christ in my heart without showing it outwardly?" he asked the evangelist.

The evangelist responded, sharing with him that all true believers must be ready to confess Christ before the world.

Pipo sat silently for a long time, thinking about his words.

The following morning he returned to his loom and his New Testament. In the years that followed, he faithfully shared the gospel with all who visited when he had the chance. He died of a fever in 1866, and on his deathbed, he urged his younger brother to promise him that he would meet him where he is going after death—heaven. Eventually, his brother, too, placed his faith in Christ and followed Pipo's example of enduring persecution.

CULTURES COLLIDE:
PAKISTAN IS BORN

For centuries, two cultures were set on a collision course. It was not a matter of *if* it would happen, but *when*.

Since Islam's arrival in Hindu-dominated India during the Middle Ages, Islam's monotheistic ideology was diametrically opposed to Hinduism's polytheistic view of religion. Muslims despised idolatry, while Hindus embraced it. Islam followed strict doctrine, while Hinduism encompassed any and all beliefs. Muslims spread their message through military strength, while Hindus used passivity to influence society. Muslims ate beef, which offended the Hindus. And Hindus ate pork, which appalled Muslims. Despite the Hindus' pacifist approach to conflict, they instigated their share of hostility by throwing pigs into mosques, and Muslims reciprocated by slaughtering cows in public.

As tensions mounted, Muslims grew increasingly discontent to live as a minority in a nation whose majority they considered infidels. All the while, Christians were caught in the middle, struggling to find their place.

In the late 1800s, unsuccessful attempts were made to reconcile the Muslim and Hindu communities in India. It was not until 1906 that Muslims organized themselves into what they called the Muslim League, which not only gave them options to end the communal strife, but also strengthened their base to make their demands heard.

Those options included the possibility of a separate Muslim state within India or a partitioning of India into Muslim India. However, when the idea was suggested of a separate state for the mostly Muslim regions of northwestern India, the Muslim community rallied, setting them on a path for nothing less than their own country with its own name.

Shortly thereafter, the proposed new country had a name. In 1933, a movement of students came up with "Pakistan," which comes from the names of the predominately Muslim areas of northwestern India: Punjab, Afghania,[4] Kashmir, Sind, and the last syllable of Baluchi*stan*. Seven years later, the Muslim League adopted the resolution making the founding of Pakistan their goal. Soon, the league was pushing for partition. All the while, the nation of India had erupted into violence.

In 1919, a British general in Amritsar, in the Punjab province, ordered a large crowd to disperse. When they failed to comply with his orders, his troops opened fire, killing more than three

---

4 Not to be confused with Afghanistan, Afghania is the Northwest Frontier Province whose residents are primarily Afghans.

hundred. However, the people were unable to leave. The general and his troops were unaware that they were blocking the crowd's only way out. The British reputation was thus damaged in India.

The violence caught the attention of Mohandas Karamchand ("Mahatma") Gandhi, an attorney who had returned to India from South Africa. Alarmed at the fighting, he united a nation of thousands of ethnic groups, pressuring Britain to "Quit India." In August 1947, not only did India win its independence through passive resistance, but Pakistan also won its place on the map, becoming a nation.

Having led the Muslim League, Mohammad Ali Jinnah took the reins of the new country and is considered the founder of Pakistan. Although India and Pakistan now had their independence,

Jinnah with Gandhi in 1944

they also had a problem: what to do with the refugees. One source says that during the nine months after partitioning, an estimated six to eight million Muslims fled predominately Hindu areas to live in Pakistan, while a similar number of Hindus and Sikhs moved to India. It is considered one of the greatest mass movements of people in history; and for the next twenty years, the resettlement of the masses would be problematic in both India and Pakistan.

In addition, Christians faced a choice: whether to live as a minority in Hindu-dominated India or in Muslim-dominated Pakistan. Most chose the latter, as many were members of lower castes (or no caste at all) and had little or no hope of a better life in India. Besides, Jinnah painted a picture of Pakistan that was appealing to minority groups. In a speech just days prior to independence, Jinnah stated, "You are free; you are free to go to your temples, you are free to go to your mosques or to any other place...in this State of Pakistan. You may belong to any religion or caste or creed that has nothing to do with the business of the State."

In his speech, he said that England, too, shared a time in history when conditions were worse than in India: Roman Catholics and Protestants persecuted each other. He continued by pointing out that countries were currently discriminating against certain classes of people. "Thank God, we are not starting in those days," he announced. "We are starting in the days where there is no discrimination, no distinction between one community and another, no discrimination between one caste or creed and another. We are starting with this fundamental principle that we are all citizens and *equal citizens of one State*" (emphasis added).

Unfortunately, not all would share in Jinnah's vision of a Pakistan for peoples of all religions as equal citizens.

Less than a year after Pakistan's birth, Jinnah died. With Christians hoping for a better life in a nation whose founder promised the freedom to worship, things turned for the worse. Successive coups would bring leaders who would take Pakistan on a different course—one that left the Christian minority concerned that their new nation was on the road to Islamization. And it all began with the wording in the country's new constitution, with good intentions gone wrong.

FREEDOM'S FAILURE:
THE RISE OF ISLAMIZATION

He promised the people freedom to worship and no discrimination based on caste or creed. But Jinnah's vision for Pakistan ended abruptly with his death, less than a year after the country was founded. One could say that any minority's hopes of thriving in this new country had died with him.

After his death, Pakistan shifted courses, causing many to question its identity: a homeland for Muslims or an Islamic state, where Shariah (Islamic law) could be enforced. In the following decades, officials would wrestle with Islam's role in the new country. As governing documents and policies were set in place, the country moved quickly toward Islamization, confirming fears among non-Muslims that an Islamic society was on the horizon.

Some believe the process of Islamization began with the adoption of the Objectives Resolution in 1949. This document assured the principles of equality, justice, free thinking, and speech, and it granted religious minorities the right to "freely profess and practice" their faith. But the Objectives Resolution went wrong with a statement that allegedly gave *carte blanche* to the furthering of Islamization in Pakistan. This controversial section stated that "Muslims should be able to order their lives in the individual and collective spheres in accordance with the teachings and requirements of Islam as set out in the Holy Quran and the Sunna."[5]

Sources say that the problem with such a statement lay in the various interpretations of Islamic law. Its ambiguity armed Islamic groups with the tools they needed to make Pakistan a Muslim country. Once again, Christians would be relegated to second-class status.

This was not the only section of the Objectives Resolution that sounded alarms for Christians and other non-Muslims. A clause stated that "sovereignty over the entire universe belongs to God Almighty alone, and the authority which He has delegated to the State of Pakistan through its people for being exercised within the limits prescribed by Him is a sacred trust." Such wording was easily interpreted by Islamic groups to mean that Pakistan was more a theocratic state than a democratic one. Others brushed off the concerns, stating the clause was just a spiritual principle with no intent to administrate politically. Many knew better.

Almost nine years after its founding, Pakistan's first constitution was finalized with the troublesome Objectives Resolution as the Pre-

---

5 The Sunna is a book recording the words and life of Mohammed.

amble. Though the constitution stated that the country was founded on Jinnah's principle of "social justice," the phrase was not defined. With the approved document, the country now had its official name—the "Islamic Republic of Pakistan"—which increasingly clued Christians and other non-Muslims in to the direction Pakistan was heading. In addition, the constitution made it clear that no non-Muslim could serve as the head of state.

In the decades that followed, the constitution would be revised repeatedly reflecting the political motives of the leader at the time. For example, President Mohammad Ayub Khan took control in a military coup in 1958 and revised the constitution in 1962, giving the appearance of a secular state while stressing Islam's authority in the country. He renamed the country the "Republic of Pakistan." However, it wasn't long until the name was changed back to the "Islamic Republic of Pakistan."

In 1973, soon after President Z. A. Bhutto took office, he renewed the focus on Islam's identity in the country by adding provisions to the constitution stating that *Islam was to be the state religion* and that the Prime Minister, too, must be a Muslim. Perhaps he and other Pakistanis realized that the British had brought India the benefit of political unity across the subcontinent, which was no longer a reality. They therefore viewed Islam as a unifying force, as echoed in the words of Professor Waheed-uz-Zahman: "If we let go the ideology of Islam, we cannot hold together as a nation by any other means."

Bhutto's revisions to the constitution were not the only indicators to Christians and other non-Muslims that their position in Pakistan was shaky. Bhutto soon enacted his nationalization program. He nationalized areas of industry, the banks, as well as agriculture, which angered land-lords, merchants, and politicians in the rural areas.

But it was his nationalization of the education system that hurt Christians most. Some Christian leaders believe his intent behind the nationalization of schools was to curb the rise of the *madrasas*, the centers of Islamic learning, since they endangered his political career. However, the nationalization policies adversely affected the schools started by missionaries, especially those helping poorer Christians. Those schools charging less than twenty rupees were taken over by the government, allowing the larger ones to remain open. Whether or not the nationalization of schools was meant to restrain the *madrasas*, some claim that they thrived and were left autonomous.

Regardless, the nationalization of schools hit the church in Pakistan hard. The damage was done.

Bhutto was soon swept out of power in a coup and replaced by General Zia ul-Haq in 1977.

Under Zia, things went from bad to worse for Christians and other non-Muslim minorities. Pakistan's process of Islamization intensified, becoming permanent in the country. Zia placed the country under martial law and pressed for legislation that legitimized Islam. Affecting the criminal justice system, he introduced Shariah benches, appointing three judges to each of Pakistan's provincial High Courts in 1978. The judges' job was to review the laws to ensure they were not abhorrent to Shariah.

A year later Zia followed up with another nail in the coffin of Jinnah's original vision for Pakistan when he propagated the dreaded Hudood Ordinances. The Hudood Ordinances are laws requiring that certain crimes be punished according to the dictates of Islam, such as stoning or flogging for adultery, fornication, rape, etc.

As if these Hudood Ordinances were not enough, through a series of constitutional amendments in 1985, the word "freely" was removed from a clause in the Objectives Resolution regarding religious liberty. What once guaranteed that religious minorities had the right to "*freely* profess and practice their religion" (emphasis added) now merely read that "an adequate provision shall be made for the minorities to profess and practice their religion and develop their culture." Pakistani Christians would agree that freedom to practice their faith has been anything but adequate. Such proof lies in the stories on the following pages. Many believe that this one small change set the stage for the proliferation of Islamic extremism in the country. One could hardly disagree when faced with repeated reports of persecution against Christians.

Inhibiting minorities' religious freedom was not Zia's final stopping point. That same year, the system of electing officials was amended establishing a procedure for separate electorates. At first Christians applauded the change, as it allowed them several representatives on the national level, giving them a voice. However, the reality of this new system quickly changed their opinion. Minorities could vote only for those minority seats reserved to represent them. For example, only Christians could vote for their small number of representatives. They could *not* vote for the Muslim majority representatives. Therefore, they could have no say in Muslims elected to office, and were subjected to those with an extreme Islamist ideology.

Zia's pro-Shariah laws and use of the military to suppress his opposition fanned the flames of violence in the streets between Muslims groups and even brought one city to the edge of civil war. All the while, Christians endured one legislative assault after another as they watched their nation change from a homeland for Muslims with hopes for a democracy to an Islamic state.

Though the Pakistani government had not targeted Christians for persecution, the increasingly Muslim policies marginalized them into second-class citizens.

Soon, a law would pass under Zia that would arm Muslims for decades to come.

WORDS OF ENDURING
WITNESS IN PAKISTAN

"How can you kill me? The Master of Life is only one and that is Jesus Christ. Only He can give or take life, so do whatever you like because I know that it is God alone who can take my life."

—BABA QADAR, 86, to a Muslim mob that raided his village of Korian in 2009

"Even if I spent twenty years in jail, I will never leave my faith."

—SANDUL BIBI, 20, who was charged under Pakistan's Blasphemy Law for desecrating a Quran (Read more about Sandul on page 93.)

"When I was being persecuted, I didn't feel their insults. I was happy to suffer for the witness of Jesus Christ. I was feeling so proud of Him I didn't realize I was in pain from the beatings. I was praying and reciting Psalm 23 in my heart, 'The Lord is my Shepherd, I will not be afraid.'"

—PARVEEN, 23, persecuted by her Muslim employers for refusing their demand to convert to Islam

"The Bible has not changed, but whoever reads it, he is changed."

—A YOUNG PAKISTANI BOY on September 17, 2007, responding to his teacher's claim that the New Testament (Injil) had been changed and contained nothing truthful. The boy was beaten by radical Muslim students.

"We are the followers of Jesus. If He says forgive your enemies, then we forgive them."

—WALTER MASIH, who lost his wife, daughter, and unborn grandchild when a Muslim mob attacked his village of Gojra in 2009

"All the time we were praying and asking Jesus to save us."

—MEHNGA MASIH, describing when his home was surrounded by a Muslim mob demanding he convert to Islam or die during a 2009 attack on his village of Korian

INTIMIDATE THE INFIDELS: THE BLASPHEMY LAW

Blasphemy: It's a crime of religious offense in Pakistan, allowing no room for disagreement with Islam. And its ambiguity has made it a powerful weapon in the hands of Muslims who wish harm to any of Pakistan's minority religious followers.

Any non-Muslim who dares to express his faith publicly in Muslim-dominated Pakistan runs the risk of breaking the country's "Blasphemy Law." The accused has everything to lose: his business, his home, even his life. But the accuser has nothing to lose. For him, it's as simple as lodging a complaint, filing a charge.

Despite Pakistani law, which does not prohibit Muslims from apostatizing or of being proselytized, the Blasphemy Law has been used by Muslims to intimidate those they consider infidels. For almost three decades, such a law has plagued the church. But its legislative roots are found in a very unlikely place that began with good intentions.

Colonial Crime

While a British colony, India was controlled by the Indian Penal Code in 1860. Chapter XV, which dealt with offenses related to religion, read that "every man should be suffered to profess his own religion, and that no man should be suffered to insult the religion of another." Those found guilty of breaking this law faced a fine or up to two years in prison.

The British authors of the code, intending to keep peace on the multi-ethnic subcontinent while protecting their business interests, further defined criminal acts against religion: "Whoever destroys, damages or defiles any place of worship, or any object, held sacred by any class of persons with the intention of thereby insulting the religion of any class of persons likely to consider such destruction, damage or defilement as an insult to their religion, shall be punished with imprisonment... or with fine or with both."

Well into the twentieth century, the law was put to the test when a Hindu writer offended India's Muslims after publishing a book on the prophet Mohammed. As a result, the British added section 295a to the Penal Code which emphasized "deliberate and malicious" intent behind angering another religious group through spoken or written words or through visibly insulting or trying to insult the religion. The Hindu writer met an end that foreshadowed the fate of other non-Muslims who violated what would later be called the Blasphemy Law: death on the streets at the hands of Muslim extremists.

Law Resurrected

During General Zia's presidency, he resurrected the law by enacting further legislation related to section 295 of Pakistan's Penal Code. Islam's supremacy in his nation was now secure.

Beginning in 1982, an amendment was passed under Zia making the willful defiling or destruction of a copy of the Quran an offense punishable by life in prison. This became section 295b.

Then in 1986, he added 295c, making it a crime to insult the prophet Mohammed. Law 295c was worse than the others: This law omitted the requirement that the perpetrator acted with malicious intent. Those found guilty of 295c faced life in prison or death. Five years later, Zia's Federal Shariat Court would find the "life in prison" allocation repugnant to Shariah Law, leaving the law's only penalty demanding death.

What has added to the volatility of the Blasphemy Law is the legal requirement involved in launching an accusation against the alleged blasphemer: Law 295a prohibits police from arresting the accused without a warrant, whereas both 295b and 295c allow police to make an arrest based on the complaint of *just one person.*

Since the early 1990s, non-Muslims—especially Christians—have been repeatedly accused of violating the Blasphemy Law. They have faced prison or been fined. As of yet, no one has been executed by the state. However, a few have been gunned down on the streets by Muslims thinking they are doing Allah a service.

The accused aren't the only ones targeted by Muslim extremists. Anyone appearing to side with them is also at risk. Judges trying the cases and lawyers representing the accused have been threatened as well. Though the Blasphemy Law was not apparently targeting any specific group in Pakistan, Christians feel the most defenseless.

No Exceptions

The Blasphemy Law has not been used primarily by Islamic purists intent on defending their religion, its holy book, and its founder. A majority of cases have involved land disputes or competing businesses with jealousy lying at the root of such accusations. In fact, the first Christian convicted under Law 295c typified this pattern.

In 1991, Gul Masih was asked by fellow villagers to repair their communal water tap. He was paid the agreed-upon fee for his services, but the water tap broke once again. One of Gul's neighbors, who was apparently a member of a militant Sunni group, questioned Gul, suspicious that the Christian had pocketed the money without fixing it. However, the neighbor's questions turned political and then religious. Soon, the intensity of their discussion drew a crowd, including Gul's brother who tried to reconcile the two. However, the neighbor had what he needed to lodge his complaint. The neighbor conspired with local Muslims and filed a complaint against both Gul and his brother. Certain that a local Muslim held a grudge after Gul confronted him for harassing women in the village, Gul sensed other motives behind his arrest.

The brothers were arrested, accused of making derogatory statements about the prophet Mohammed and his wife Aisha while criticizing local *moulanas* (Muslim teachers) for indulging in adultery. But according to Gul's brother, no blasphemous comments were ever made during the course of the heated dialogue. Rather, one of the local Muslims concocted the charges to get elected to a local office.

How the courts handled Gul's case reflects the Islamization that has pervaded the legal system.

Police found Gul's brother innocent and released him, but not Gul. Even though the police admitted there was no evidence in his case to substantiate the charges, they were not allowed to release him. What didn't help matters was the animosity stirred up among the citizens. The town erupted in demonstrations with posters calling for the death of both brothers. Lawyers wouldn't accept the case, knowing the risk it posed for their own lives. However, the Human Rights Commission of Pakistan finally stepped in and represented him.

When Gul finally appeared in court, two of the witnesses for the prosecution admitted that there were no blasphemies uttered against the prophet Mohammed or his wife Aisha. The only accuser who insisted on such remarks was Gul's neighbor. The judge rendered his verdict, words of mockery to Jinnah's vision of Pakistan. He declared that since Gul's neighbor was a man of a certain age with a beard and the disposition of being a true Muslim, he had no reason to disbelieve him. To the judge, the prosecution had proved the case against Gul beyond a reasonable doubt. With that, Gul was sentenced to death but not before paying a fine of five thousand rupees.

The death sentence was appealed and Gul was acquitted by the Lahore High Court in 1994. However, he was a marked man in a Muslim-dominated society convinced that he had blasphemed their prophet. He fled to Europe for safety.

Some Christians accused of blasphemy did not have the opportunity to find safety in another country. In 1992, eighty-year-old Bantu Masih was arrested for blasphemy and was stabbed by his accuser while in police custody. He later died from the stab wounds.

More recently, a Christian named Imran Masih was accused of desecrating the Quran (violating section 295b) and offending the religion of Islam (section 295a) in July 2009. His accuser, Haji Liaqat, was a competitor of Imran's family business as well as a member of an Islamic extremist group.

On July 1, Imran was burning old school papers, and pages of the Quran were among those papers. Imran's intention was not malicious or meaning to offend Haji and other Muslims. According to Imran, the pages were among poorly completed school papers that were a disgrace to him. Some of the papers managed to fly out of the shop and into Haji's possession. Instead of confronting Imran and asking him about the pages, Haji stirred up the town, accusing Imran of desecrating the Quran. Imran and his father were both beaten. Police showed up and arrested Imran, but the crowds of offended Muslims were far from being appeased. They took to the streets, marching with signs saying, "Give death sentence!"

Rioting from Imran's case

and "Hang him who disgraces the Quran!" They shouted, "Christians are dogs!" and made an image of Imran and hanged it. Imran was sentenced to life in prison and fined 100,000 rupees.

Women are also not exempt from accusations of blasphemy.

Thirty-seven-year-old Asia Bibi was arrested by police in June 2009 for blasphemy and was given the death penalty. As a worker on a farm owned by a Muslim, Asia was pressured by many of her female coworkers to renounce Christianity and accept Islam.

One day the pressure became especially strong during an intense discussion among the women about their faith. Asia responded by sharing with them about Christ. She told her Muslim coworkers that Jesus died on the cross for our sins. Then

Asia Bibi

apparently she asked them what Mohammed had done for them. "Our Christ is the true prophet of God," she reportedly told them, "and yours is not true."

Infuriated with Asia, the Muslim women beat her until a group of men took her away and locked her in a room. They announced from mosque loudspeakers that she would be punished: her face would be blackened and she would be paraded through the village on a donkey. Local Christians informed the police, who took Asia into custody before the Muslims could carry out their plan. Christians had urged the police not to file blasphemy charges, but police claimed that they must proceed due to pressure from local Muslim leaders.

On November 8, 2010, a judge convicted Asia of blasphemy and sentenced her to death. If carried out, she will be the first woman to be executed for blasphemy. Since her conviction, many developments have taken place in her case, leaving it open for change when this book goes to

Asia's family

press. An appeal is planned, but no date has been set for the hearing. Days after her sentence was issued, reports circulated that President Zardari was considering pardoning Asia. However, the Lahore High Court ruled that the president can not pardon her before her appeal to the High Court is decided.

As she wades through the tedious judicial process, she has received numerous death threats. A hard-line imam offered $6,000 to anyone who kills her. Even a government official trying to advocate on her behalf was targeted. On January 4, 2011, the governor of Punjab Province, Salman Taseer, was killed by his own bodyguard for speaking against the blasphemy laws. He had recently visited Asia in jail. Finally, in February 2011, the government of Pakistan ruled that it would not amend the blasphemy laws after nationwide protests against revising the law.

The governor would not be the only official silenced. On March 2, 2011, Pakistan's Prime Minister of Minority Affairs, Shahbaz Bhatti, was assassinated on his way to work. Bhatti, the first Christian to be appointed to a cabinet position, also urged Pakistan to reform the blasphemy laws. Just a month before his death, Bhatti visited Ottawa, Canada, to meet with Canadian Prime Minister Stephen Harper. "I've faced assassination attempts; I've been in prison," said Bhatti in a Toronto Sun article. "I'm told by the extremists that if I will continue to speak out, I can be killed," he shared.

Despite protesting the draconian Blasphemy Law, little to nothing has occurred. However, as news of Christians accused of blasphemy have reached the West, many have responded by writing letters to the accused as well as Pakistani officials asking for the law's repeal. It is believed some of the acquittals have resulted from such grassroots efforts.

In addition to the single accusations of blasphemy, entire villages have faced mob violence due to such charges, the first occurring in the late 1990s with the village of Shanti Nagar.

SIDEBAR:
RAMADAN

Every year Muslims around the globe observe the holiday called *Ramadan*, the ninth month of the Islamic calendar, which is based on the lunar cycle. Therefore, when compared to the conventional Gregorian calendar, the dates of Ramadan will change each year, just as the dates of Easter vary annually based on the moon.

Ramadan comes from the Arabic word *ramida* or *ar-ramad*, meaning extreme heat and aridness, specifically related to the earth. Likening the meaning of "Ramadan" to the heat from the sun, some believe that month is a time when sins are burned out with good deeds.

The primary activity during Ramadan is fasting. From dawn until dusk, Muslims refrain from food, drink, and other pleasures, believing such abstinence shows their submission to God and serves as penance for their sins. At sunset, Muslims break the fast with a meal called *iftar*. This will continue for thirty days.

Fasting during Ramadan is one of the five basic tenets, or pillars, of Islam.[6] The first is reciting the Muslim creed, or *Shahada*, "There is no

---

6 These pillars reflect Sunni Islam. Shia Islam observes pillars that are less practical in terms of actions and more abstract.

god but Allah, and Mohammed is his prophet." The second is prayer, or *Salat*, five times a day. Third is almsgiving, or *Zakat*, meaning helping the poor. Fourth is observing the fast, or *Sawm*, during Ramadan; and fifth is going on the *Hajj*, or pilgrimage, to Mecca, where Islam began. Some have added a sixth pillar, which is *jihad*, meaning "holy war" or "struggle." This bears the idea of bringing others into the Islamic religion through persuasion or compulsion.

Ramadan is significant to Muslims, as they believe it was during this time that the Quran was first revealed to the prophet Mohammed. On the first night of Ramadan, many Muslims will be looking to the sky for the crescent moon, an Islamic symbol.[7] Called the "night of power," the twenty-seventh night is believed to be when Mohammed received his first revelation of the Quran in A.D. 610 in a cave near Mecca. During this time, mosques are teeming with people offering

---

7 The crescent moon as a worship symbol actually precedes Islam and was used by Eastern peoples in their worship along with the sun and sky gods. It is believed that the crescent moon and star became associated with Islam during the Ottoman Empire. According to legend, Osman, who founded the Ottoman Empire, had a dream where he saw the crescent moon stretch from one end of the earth to the other. He viewed it as a good sign and therefore adopted it as an emblem for his dynasty. However, some Muslims reject the crescent moon, saying Islam has no symbol and should not use a previously pagan image.

prayers during the night, as many believe Allah is more receptive to their pleas and there is an increase in visions and miracles. Ramadan ends on a day called *Eid-ul-Fitr*, when many visit friends and family, dress up, and exchange gifts.

DESECRATION AND DESTRUCTION: MOB VIOLENCE

It was Ramadan's "night of power"—the time when Muslims believe Mohammed had received his first revelation from the angel Gabriel in A.D. 610. The mosques were filled with faithful followers who had gathered, prepared to spend much of the night in prayer, believing Allah is more receptive to their cries for help on this particular night. But for the residents of Shanti Nagar, February 5, 1997, would be remembered as a night that a Muslim mob showed its power in reaction to allegations of a Quran being desecrated.

The rumblings began a month earlier, when a sixty-year-old Christian named Raji Baba was arrested on January 14, on suspicions of managing a gambling operation and alcohol distillery. As the police searched his home, one of them dropped a Bible on the floor. Though Raji begged the officer to pick it up, he disregarded his pleas and kicked it, then dragged him to the station.

Word got out about Raji's arrest and the Bible kicking. Christians went to the station to appeal his release and register a case against the officers responsible for "desecrating" the Bible. Raji was released, but their case was ignored.

Furious, Christians took to the street on January 17. Their protest worked, or perhaps seemed to work, as officials planned to arrest the officers who kicked Raji's Bible. But before the perpetrators could be arrested, they managed to secure bail for themselves.

In a matter of days, the Christians saw the guilty officers back on duty. Again, they organized a protest insisting the officers be immediately dismissed and charges filed under Section 295a. (The charges were filed under what Pakistan calls a "First Information Report" [FIR], meaning the evidence submitted is admissible as evidence. After an FIR is filed, the investigation can begin.) Once filed, the police officer primarily responsible for kicking the Bible was discharged.

Once again peace settled over the area of Shanti Nagar and the neighboring Tibba Colony. Up to this time, Christians had a history of living harmoniously with Muslims in their villages. But their restored peace was short-lived.

On the night of February 5, many Muslims had crowded into the area mosques to commemorate Ramadan's night of power. Then at 10:30 p.m., a shout rang out from the mosque at Jamia Masjid Gapwal-Khanewal. The voice declared that pages of the Quran with blasphemous words written on them were found torn up and burned near a bridge, just 2.5 kilometers from Shanti

Nagar. The person who supposedly committed the act? Raji Baba.

It didn't matter that both Christians and Muslims questioned the accusation, many Muslims were angry. Soon word spread of the alleged blasphemy, and residents were called upon to raid Shanti Nagar and other Christian communities to take revenge.

And they did.

In a matter of moments, the mob grew into the thousands. But before they arrived in Shanti Nagar, police stopped them, at least for the night.

The following morning the mob had grown to 20,000 to 30,000, and they set their sights on Shanti Nagar. They arrived at 9:00 a.m. Outnumbered, the police withdrew. The residents of Shanti Nagar were on their own, left to defend themselves against the anger of the shouting mass of Muslims, some of whom carried posters calling for the death of Christians, blasphemers against the Quran.

Armed with rocks, knives, axes, firearms, and explosives, the mob looted and burned homes. They cut off telephones and electricity, damaged the village's water pumps and tanks, and drove their livestock away. But worse, they kidnapped many women, who were forcibly converted and some even raped.

The violence and destruction finally stopped when the army got involved. But it was too late.

More than seven hundred of the nine hundred homes, including four churches, in Shanti Nagar and surrounding settlements were destroyed. In addition, an estimated 2,500 Christians were forced to flee.

Some believe the violence was planned and orchestrated by the dismissed police officer who had kicked Raji Baba's Bible. It should be noted that in the end, Raji's alleged gambling and alcohol accusations were unsubstantiated.

The brutality that hit Shanti Nagar was the first time a mob had attacked as a result of blasphemy charges. And it wouldn't be the last.

More than twelve years later, the villages of Korian and Gojra, both in the Punjab province, would face the same destruction, and it would happen after an accusation of blasphemy.

The violence in Korian began when a boy had allegedly cut up pages of an Arabic textbook that contained words from the Quran. The cut-up pages were used as confetti at a Christian wedding. But apparently, Muslims already had a long-standing grudge with the boy's father, and some speculate that the incident at the wedding may have been an opportunity to snatch the Christians' land, which had become valuable since the government had apportioned it between the Muslims and Christians years earlier.

The area mosque announced that Christians had disgraced the Quran and Muslims should kill them. One pastor said that the mosque was calling Muslims to come with their weapons and was threatening to burn Christians' homes. Armed with guns and explosives, the mob quickly grew to eight hundred. Witnesses say some of the attackers included members of radical organizations linked to the Taliban and al-Qaeda.

One Christian man named Mehnga Masih was locked in his house with his wife and nine children when the mob came.

"Convert to Islam or die!" shouted the mob outside his home.

Frightened, Mehnga and his family did the only thing they could do: pray. Soon, their prayers were answered. Managing to flee their home, they hid in the long grass as they watched homes in their village of Korian go up in flames.

But the terror did not end at Korian's borders. Two days later in the neighboring village of Gojra, the growing mob attacked. Mosque loudspeakers fanned the flames of violence proclaiming, "Kill the . . . dogs."

Christians cried out for help from police, but the small number who responded were no match for the well-armed attackers. When more police arrived, the mob opened fire on the Christians' protectors.

In a matter of hours, a hundred homes were burned and seven Christians were killed.

Among the dead were Walter Masih's wife, grown daughter, and her unborn child. "We are very scared," he told a worker from VOM's sister mission, Britain's Release International. "These people can attack again whenever they want. We can do nothing—only believe in Jesus. We have a strong trust in Him."

Unfortunately, the violence will likely not end with the brutality in Shanti Nagar, Korian, and Gojra. Still, many Christians are clinging to the words of Jesus and living them out through His grace as further attacks could be unleashed at any time—it's simply a matter of time, opportunity, and motive. In recent years such hostility has come not only from Muslims seeking to take revenge or to undercut successful business competitors, but also from radical Islamic groups.

TESTIMONY:
A MEMBER OF THE TALIBAN
TURNS TO CHRIST

"Rafiq" (not his real name) had learned about Christ through a correspondence course, but a Muslim teacher warned him that Christian books were from "infidels." Though he quit the course, he did not forget about Jesus. After becoming a medical doctor, he joined a training camp where he learned how to be a terrorist. Here he shares his testimony of how he turned to Christ.

I traveled to Afghanistan, to a remote city. There I joined a radical Islamic training camp. I spent nine months in that camp and received all kinds of terrorist training from the Taliban.

When I came back to Pakistan, I joined another radical Islamic training camp in the Northwest Frontier Province (NWFP). This training camp belongs to Jash-e-Muhammad.[8] The head of this organization is a *moulana* [Muslim teacher].

Early in the morning there were different physical exercises. Then, after breakfast there were classes. This was a kind of brainwashing session. After that they taught us how to make bombs

---

8 In 2001, Jash-e-Muhammad was involved in the Bahawalpur church attack, killing sixteen innocent people.

and hand grenades. Then we practiced how to detonate the bombs. They had all kinds of weapons. They taught us how to operate Kalashnikovs [assault rifles], pistols, and rocket launchers. They also taught us how to destroy trains and hijack airplanes. We learned bank robbery and how to disrupt traffic. They also taught us how to murder, how to torture people, and how to execute suicide bombings. I learned everything, but I was against killing people. I am a doctor by profession; our job is to save lives, not to kill.

Before 9/11, when I was in Afghanistan for twenty-four days working with the Taliban, they kidnapped a foreigner from Europe. One day, I was called in for his medical checkup because his blood pressure was very high. The leader of our gang said, "This man is a Christian and is preaching in Afghanistan. He is distributing Christian literature among Afghans. He is not able to receive forgiveness. We will kill him." I was against his killing and clashed with them, but later they killed him. This was the turning point of my life. I was thinking, *What was this man preaching? What does his religion say?* Again I started studying about Christianity.

After 9/11, I was working with the Red Cross in Afghanistan. I met some Christian workers and found some literature. I had thought Americans were animals. They are killing people, and they are fighting in our country. But when I was caught in Afghanistan, and met the Red Cross people who were foreigners and saved my life, I began thinking, *We want to kill them, and they are saving our lives.* When I returned to Pakistan, I looked for some Christian leaders. In 2003, I asked one to provide me with some Christian literature. During this time I accepted Christ. I began to distribute hundreds of Bibles among Muslims in schools, mosques, and different villages.

I have received many threatening calls from the Taliban and local Muslim leaders. They tell me, "Do not distribute the Christian literature. Otherwise, we will kill you." The Taliban killed my friend who was dressed like me and driving my car. The terrorist thought I was in that vehicle.

I know terrorists have lots of weapons and can kill me, and they can kill anybody. I can also kill, but I cannot kill. If I kill my enemies, what difference will there be between them and me? If they kill us, the work and the Word will spread. They will kill, and we will work. I am not afraid of death. One night three radical Muslims came into my hotel room and tried to kill me as I slept, but God saved my life. I was injured, but I am getting better.

When I was young, there were some people who gave a speech in our school that the Taliban were the saviors of the world, and they will give you the right way to follow Allah. I befriended members of al-Qaeda, and I am ashamed of that.

I feel guilty because so many innocent people were killed, and I trained so many young people for *jihad* and that was a sin. God forgive me.

In 1998, I met Osama bin Laden. I introduced myself, and he was very happy to see me. He said to me, "This is very good that you came to the camp. We need young people like you."

I was impressed because he was a big leader and I had met him. Now I think he is a big enemy of human beings. In their religion, they say they do not kill innocent people, but the people they killed in the training camp were innocent people. Osama is no hero. He did not bring his son, his brother, his own family members for *jihad*.

I feel shame in me and very guilty about all kinds of things I have done. I don't know what kind of spirit was forcing me to do that, but now there is another Spirit behind what I do.

We were told if someone changes his religion —kill him. If someone leaves his faith and believes in freedoms—kill him. Although I changed my religion, I am not a *kafir* (an apostate or infidel). *Kafirs* do not believe in God, but I believe in God.

The Bible can change any type of person. The plan was given to me to kill Americans, Christians—all kinds of people. But I was changed so other people can be changed. I have a strong faith in Christ, and I have accepted Jesus as Savior of my life.

RADICAL ROOTS: THE "TALIBANIZATION" OF PAKISTAN

The Christians of the Taiser colony in Karachi had been warned. Members of the Taliban scrawled threats on the outside of churches and Christians' homes in April 2009. "Convert to Islam or pay the *jizya!*"[9] said one. "Long live the Taliban!" said another. Encroaching on the country's financial center, the Taliban was after total control and total submission to Islam.

In response to the graffiti, Christians demonstrated, pleading with authorities for protection. But their request was ignored, leaving the outnumbered Christians to fend for themselves.

Days later, as the Christians were cleaning off the graffiti, armed men tried to stop them. Some say that others arrived on the scene and began firing on the crowd. When police showed up, they arrested several suspects. However, reports indicate that members of the Taliban had already arrived in the colony. Dragging Christians out of

---

9 The *jizya* is a high poll tax levied on non-Muslims who refuse to convert to Islam, ensuring their physical protection. The *jizya* is linked to what is called *dhimma* status, a treaty agreement between Muslim conquerors and the non-Muslim conquered peoples. For more information on the *dhimma*, see *Restricted Nations: Iran.*

their homes at gunpoint, they shouted at them, calling them infidels, demanding they convert to Islam or die. It became apparent that they were going to make good on their threats. "Why did you clean off the warnings?" they shouted at Christians. "How dare you stage a protest against the Taliban?"

A militant movement consisting predominantly of Pashtun insurgents who were forced out of Afghanistan in 2001, the Taliban mob burned three churches and dozens of Christian businesses in Taiser. One report shares that dozens were injured and one Christian was shot execution style.

Some say the Taiser attack is a warning to the local government about the Taliban's motives to expand Shariah into Karachi. Just a week before the attack, President Asif Ali Zardari had struck a deal, allowing Shariah law to be administered in Swat Valley by Muslim leaders linked to the Taliban. Those in favor of the agreement say the Taliban committed to stop their violence in exchange for Shariah in the Malakand division in Pakistan's Northwest Frontier Province, which borders Afghanistan and

President Asif Ali Zardari

is a harbor for terrorist groups. Opponents of Zardari's compromise say it only served to bolster the Taliban, giving them *carte blanche* to push for more autonomy and control in other areas of Pakistan. Given the great distance between Karachi and Swat Valley (approximately 1,000 km or about 700 miles), the attack on Taiser shows the Taliban's intent to spread its influence beyond the section neighboring Afghanistan.

For some Christians, the threats from radical Islamic groups have been more personal than graffiti on the wall.

The "Talwar" family of Punjab province received a letter from al-Qaeda elements, ordering them to leave within a week or face death. "Allah is one and beside him there is no other God who is merciful and forgives...We know you people and the activities you are involved in," the letter stated. "You are also preaching the gospel here. Therefore, you are asked to leave this country in one week. Otherwise, we will kill you and your people."

The family did not move. Instead, they asked for prayer: "Pray that God will sustain us, provide us accommodation, and protect us from the schemes of our enemies."

Months prior to Zardari's agreement and the April 2009 attack on Taiser, the area of Swat Valley was fast becoming a Taliban stronghold. In January, the Taliban banned the education of girls.

More than one hundred schools for girls were forced to close, some of which were bombed or burned. Taliban members took to the airwaves, warning girls that if they dared attend school, they could be attacked with acid. Teachers were also threatened with death.

The restrictions on females were not confined to education. The Taliban also ruled that women and girls were to wear full veils, and women had to be accompanied by male family members when venturing out in public. A dozen women were reportedly shot for committing alleged immoral acts. Public executions even became commonplace. Despite Pakistan's parliament unanimously voting to condemn the Taliban's school closings in Swat Valley, one source questioned if government officials would commit to making sure the schools are reopened or remain in a state of inaction.

In essence, the Pakistani government had a problem: how would it turn the Taliban tide and keep the movement from spreading?

The April 2009 agreement by Zardari stirred up international outrage. Just weeks later, the government ended the deal, instead committing to ridding the country, specifically Swat Valley, of Taliban forces.

Many wonder why Zardari would strike a deal with the Taliban, considering the Taliban's bent toward being "unappeasable" and the group's radical element of implementing Shariah. In addition, his late wife, Benazir Bhutto, was critical of the Blasphemy Law's harsh punishment. Amid this very unstable political situation in the region bordering Afghanistan, some speculate that Zardari's deal was a gesture to appease the Taliban.

The growing radical element in Pakistan has been behind several cases of Christian persecution since 9/11. In June 2008, Salamat Masih and thirty of his family members and friends faced the fury of a Taliban Islamist group called Lashka-e-Islam in the community of Academy Town in the Peshawar province. As they had gathered to celebrate the birth of his daughter and pray, a dozen members of the extremist group burst into his home and held the Christians at gunpoint. Salamat's landlord was also present at the time of the raid to collect his rent.

The sixteen men at the celebration were taken and held captive for an hour. Their persecutors beat the men, while shouting at them to convert to Islam. The men refused. They were then taken to a cave, but were released ten hours later.

Apparently, there are a hundred Christian families living in an area of Academy Town that used to be a *madrasa* (Muslim school). A local Muslim renovated the school, converting it into smaller homes and renting them out to Christians, like Salamat. A week before the birth celebration raid, members of Lashkar-e-Islam approached the landlord and ordered him to evict all Christian families, saying, "Christians should not reside, pray, or celebrate in a place that was formerly a *madrasa*."

The Taliban's threats have not been confined to Muslims. They affect any religious minority, including the Sikhs, followers of Sikhism, a belief founded in India. In February 2010, the Taliban abducted three Sikhs and held them for ransom. One of them was murdered. Abductions by the Taliban are not uncommon. One report relates that members of the Taliban are allegedly using criminal activities such as kidnappings and robbery to raise funds for their movement.

As radical elements like the Taliban bully their way through Pakistan to establish Shariah and a form of *dhimma*, Christians and other non-Muslim minorities are left vulnerable. In an article on Dawn.com, an English newspaper of Pakistan, U.S.-based attorney Rafia Zakaria writes, "At the heart of the problem lies the assurance that the lives of minorities who are crushed between the barbarity of the Taliban and the corruption of the state are ultimately expendable and unworthy of protection."

Despite their precarious temporal position, Christians in Pakistan are embracing their eternal standing before Christ as members of His kingdom.

STORY FROM TODAY:
EXTREMIST EVANGELIST

"Qabil" (not his real name) and his wife heard the knock at the door. Neither was prepared for what awaited them.

Qabil opened the door and stepped outside to speak with the unannounced guests. Soon they would learn why the men, members of the Taliban, were there.

"We told you many times not to preach," they shouted at the evangelist while hitting his stocky frame, "but you didn't stop! Now we'll teach you a lesson!"

His wife quietly listened through the door as she heard the verbal abuse and her husband's groans of pain.

Then the men shoved Qabil into a waiting vehicle and sped off.

Qabil had chosen to move his family to one of the most unsettled areas of his country—Pakistan's Northwest Frontier Province, where members of al-Qaeda and the Taliban have taken refuge since being ousted from Afghanistan in the war after 9/11. Here, he shared the gospel, but his evangelistic efforts caught the attention of the extremists who wanted him silenced.

Qabil's wife was distraught at his kidnapping. She hid her children and phoned fellow believers, crying for help. She was the only Christian in the village. Who else could she turn to? Soon, her plea for prayer spread across the globe.

The Taliban drove Qabil to their training camp and put him in a basement where for two hours they hung him upside down inside a squat toilet. As the blood rushed to his head, Qabil recited Psalm 23 and prayed to God, asking for strength to endure the torture and to be released.

The Taliban was not finished with Qabil. They showed him pictures of Christian leaders and asked him to identify them. They also wanted to know who was working with this infidel who dared to turn people away from Islam.

Finally, they beat his naked body and locked him in the bathroom for the night.

At 4:15 a.m., Qabil's prayers were answered. A man he knew opened the door and signaled to him to escape. More than two hours later, he was home.

The following day, Qabil and his family fled the area.

"I was afraid," shared Qabil, "but when I ... heard that people were praying for me, I was encouraged ... That moment, I decided to go back and preach in the same area. My fear is gone."

JILTED JUSTICE:
ACTS AGAINST WOMEN

Treated as second-class citizens, Christians in Pakistan are harassed, falsely accused, and beaten. One wonders, can it get any worse?

The answer: Yes, it can.

For Christian women in Pakistan, the cases of violence against them are countless. One doesn't have to go far to read the numerous incidents of abuse, abduction, rape, and forced marriages. Many more women remain quiet about their ordeals, knowing they will either be ignored by a legal system that favors the Muslim majority, or face charges of *zina* (adultery).

Though justice is no friend to Christian women in Pakistan, many have tried to help the victims and have paid dearly for doing so. And some women have survived their ordeal and now tell their story. One is Shafia.

Shafia grew up in a Christian family. But her father died in 1990, leaving her mother, sister, and two brothers in a struggle to survive. Her brother Rafia went to work in a cotton factory to support the family, but he vocally objected to the treatment of Christian women by Muslims in his community—and it cost him. He was drugged and then shot in the head.

Having lost their main provider a second time, Shafia and her family were devastated. In order to bring Rafia's murderers to justice, the family was required to pay to have them prosecuted. Selling their house, livestock, and land to lodge their case, the family filed charges. But two years later, the court demanded more money. Shafia's family couldn't pay.

Having heard of Rafia's case, a Muslim man named Masood offered to help Shafia's family fund the court fees. He gave Shafia some papers to sign and said he needed her signature to proceed with the prosecution.

Soon, rumors spread through the village that Shafia and Masood had married. The papers that Masood had given her to sign were not for the case but for a marriage certificate.

Christian and Muslim leaders in the village met and negotiated, causing Muslim leaders to pressure Masood to sign a divorce agreement. In the end, the marriage was dissolved.

Though the fabricated marriage had ended, Masood's anger ignited.

Three days later, Masood took revenge. As Shafia and her mother were walking through a field, the sound of an approaching motorcycle caught their attention. It was Masood. Leaping off his motorcycle, he pulled out a pistol and fired a shot into the air. He pushed Shafia's mother to the ground. After hitting Shafia, he dragged her to his motorcycle. "If you speak, I'll shoot you," he threatened as she felt the barrel of the pistol press into her back.

He drove her to his house and threw her into a room on the top floor where she was his captive for four months. Every night was the same: He raped her. He beat her. He demanded she convert to Islam. Despite the shame and physical pain, she remained faithful to Jesus, telling Masood, "I am a Christian, and if you want to kill me then kill me, but I will not accept Islam."

Every day Shafia checked the door. One day, it paid off. Masood forgot to lock it. She managed to escape and ran back to her family.

Now the family was faced with another need for justice. Borrowing U.S. $217 from a brick kiln owner, they filed a case against Masood. However, instead of seeing the man who had kidnapped and violated Shafia be convicted of his crimes, the family became indentured slaves at a brickyard, working twelve-hour days, making a meager U.S. $3 for every one thousand bricks they had made. While Shafia and her family made bricks, her heart healed as she read Scriptures about forgiving one's persecutors. Soon, VOM heard of her case and paid to free the family from slavery and help the family become self-supporting.

Unfortunately, not all cases end like Shafia's. Some of the victims are just children.

Twelve-year-old Shazia Bashir Masih died from malnutrition and physical abuse in January 2010. Working as a domestic employee for Muslim attorney Chaudhary Muhammad Naeem, Shazia earned approximately a thousand rupees a month (about U.S. $12), providing the only income for her family. Naeem refused to let Shazia see her family.

Three months prior to her death, Naeem finally conceded and let her visit her family. During her visit, she told them that Naeem and his family were beating and raping her. Shazia's mother and uncle went to the police for help, but were told that a case against an attorney was unthinkable.

Shazia's physical condition worsened, and Naeem let her go home. She was hospitalized and died of malnourishment three days later. The initial medical report listed her cause of death as the "misuse of medicine," as well as malnourishment and physical injuries. Thirteen of her wounds were identified as coming from a blunt instrument and five from a sharp-edged weapon.

Then just two months later, twenty-year-old Kiran George and her unborn child died after her Muslim employer's son poured gasoline over her and set her on fire. She was pregnant with his child.

The abduction and rape of women is most common in rural areas, as the women are usually from poor families and must work to help provide income. This requires them to be in the fields and homes of Muslim employers where anything can happen and no one can hear them cry for help.

Pakistan's legal system has set the stage for such failures of justice for Christian women. With the Hudood Ordinances approved during General Zia's presidency, a Christian woman's testimony holds only one-fourth the clout of that of a Muslim man. However, during Musharraf's presidency (2001–2008), the Women's Protection Bill was passed, eliminating portions of the Hudood Ordinances. One welcome change from the bill ordered that rape cases be tried by criminal law versus Islamic law. However, the reform did not end all atrocities, such as honor killings.

In addition to such Hudood hindrances, both Islamic Shariah law and Pakistani law state that the conversion of a Christian woman to Islam requires the automatic dissolution of her marriage to her Christian husband. Therefore, when Christian women are kidnapped, their captors force them to recite the *Shahada* (Muslim creed) to "convert" them, and then they are forced to marry their captors. Although some women have publicly admitted to their new marriage and conversion to Islam, some believe this is only because the women fear what will happen if they tell the truth.

Nineteen-year-old Sonia Mohan was tricked into leaving her home by a Muslim named Ali

Raza in April 2010. Her family fears that she will be forced to convert to Islam and then marry him. If she becomes pregnant, justice and any type of normalcy for the young woman will be nearly impossible. One source notes that police will often delay the investigation until after the kidnapped woman becomes pregnant, as allegedly it is legally unheard of for a court to return a pregnant young woman or girl to her family.

Some judges have occasionally tried to help. In 1991, a lower court in Faisalabad ruled that in such abduction cases a woman's conversion was not sincere, given that the kidnapper had committed a crime. However, a year later, the decision was overturned in a higher court based on Shariah. Apparently, the sincerity of any conversion to Islam is not to be questioned.

Many also believe that rape has been used as a way to punish a family or teach the family a lesson, explaining why some police have been known to use rape to intimidate women of lower classes in Pakistan.

Despite the lack of justice, God is bringing healing in the lives of Christian women who have faced the shame and violence of rape and beatings. Parveen, who was held by her Muslim employers because she refused to work for them on a Sunday, clung to Jesus as she was tortured. "I didn't feel their insults," she shared. "I was happy to suffer for the witness of Jesus Christ. I was feeling so proud of Him I didn't realize I was in pain from the beatings. I was praying and reciting Psalm 23 in my heart, 'The Lord is my Shepherd, I will not be afraid.'"

Many believe that pressure from the media and human rights organizations push police to pursue cases of rape and kidnappings. Pray that God will continue to use such groups to help Christian women in Pakistan, while asking Him to bring complete healing in their hearts and minds. Ask the Lord to instill in each Pakistani woman a sense of dignity that they are created in His image and that they will each fully realize their gifting and calling (Genesis 1:27; Romans 11:29).

Though justice is denied, it's only temporary. May we be faithful in our prayers and actions to help Christian women in Pakistan until the day of Christ's return, when true justice will be realized.

A GLIMPSE OF JUSTICE: SANDUL BIBI'S STORY

The evidence was planted. Torn pages of the Quran were found near twenty-year-old Sandul Bibi's home, where she lived with her parents. Word soon spread. Mosque loudspeakers accused Christians of desecrating the Quran, calling on Muslims to attack. They did.

They threw rocks and fired guns at Christians in a church and then honed in on their target: Sandul.

With their home surrounded, Sandul and her family huddled together as they heard rocks pelt the side of their house. Instead of giving in to fear, Sandul comforted her parents, reading from the Sermon on the Mount.

Sandul and her father, Gulsher

Police showed up. But instead of protecting Sandul and her parents from the violent mob, police arrested her and her father, Gulsher, and charged them with violating Law 295b of Pakistan's Penal Code: blaspheming the Quran.

Facing a possible four-year prison sentence, Sandul and her father were held for eleven months without a trial. During that time, she received a Bible and a copy of *Tortured for Christ* by VOM founder Richard Wurmbrand. She needed the encouragement. During the month of Ramadan, Muslims told her she needed to pray with them, but she refused. "I am a Christian," she replied. "I pray to Jesus Christ. Why should I say prayers with you? I will not do that."

When she felt lonely, she prayed to the Lord and sensed His presence. "I talk with God," she shared. "In the presence of God I feel strengthened and peace of mind. I am happy that this way God fulfills His Words that 'I am with you.'"

Finally, in December 2009, after she and her father had endured more than forty separate court hearings, they were released. The charges of desecrating the Quran were proven to be false—a glimpse of justice. Upon their release, they were taken to a secure place to be reunited with their family.

CONCLUSION:
A BETTER COUNTRY

They were given the assurance of a better country, one that was for all peoples and all religions. But what Pakistan became was not what Christians and other non-Muslims were promised. Even the country's flag, whose white band represents minorities, appears as nothing but a reminder of the freedom they were supposed to have but don't.

After the nationalization of schools in 1972, many talked of a separate Christian country called *Takistan*. But for the small percentage of Christians, that idea was merely a dream, a hope that would likely never happen. Years following the organization of the Pakistani Christian Congress in 1985, some began to suggest a province of their own. Still, many said this was unlikely.

Despite facing disappointment and mourning the loss of what was supposed to be, a segment of Christians have made a choice: they are seeking a better country, that is, a heavenly one (Hebrews 11:16). They follow a God who is not ashamed of their lowly earthly status. At times, they are discouraged; at others, they are rejoicing. They have been beaten, imprisoned, raped, and some gunned down on the streets.

They are risking their lives to take the gospel to their fiercest enemies: the Taliban and other Islamic extremist groups. They refuse to give in to their Muslim employers who pressure them—and even beat them—to convert to Islam. And they endure the false accusations of blaspheming Islam, the Quran, and Mohammed that have been lodged against them by jealous Muslims nursing more than a grudge.

All the while, their feet remain steadfast, heading in the same direction: toward their eternal country with Jesus.

In the spirit of Hebrews 10:33, you can become companions of those who are mistreated. The Voice of the Martyrs offers many opportunities to encourage and help our persecuted family in Pakistan. Through prisoneralert.com, you can write letters of encouragement to Christians who are sitting in prison on false blasphemy charges. Sandul Bibi received thousands of letters while she endured over forty court appearances.

VOM's Action Pack program has helped Christians forced to flee their homes in areas of Pakistan where they face the rising threat of Islamic extremism. Filled with items such as blankets, clothing, and toiletries by Christians across the U.S., Action Packs have been a simple way to give out of our abundance and show Christians in Pakistan that they are not forgotten.

VOM also has several funds that enable the ministry to send financial help to families whose primary breadwinner was imprisoned or killed, as well as print Christian literature and Scriptures in Urdu to encourage believers to stand firm.

And finally, you can pray. Pray that the Blasphemy Law will be repealed. Pray that Christians in Pakistan will continue sharing the gospel boldly. Ask God to give women who are abused by their Muslim employers a means to make a living where they are no longer subjected to such violence. And pray that the Lord continues to use their enduring witness to bring their persecutors into a relationship with Jesus Christ.

We invite you to join your brothers and sisters in Pakistan. May their enduring witness inspire you to pursue more than a temporal social utopia but a better, more heavenly country that awaits those who have placed their faith in Christ!

TIMELINE OF EVENTS

The following timeline reflects numerous events highlighted in this book.

Circa A.D. 70   Apostle Thomas martyred.

711   Arabs led by General Muhammad bin Qasim conquer Sind in northwestern India.

1001   Turks invade led by Mahmud of Gazni.

1525   Babur invades; the following year, the Mughal Empire is established.

1579   Three Jesuits leave to join Mughal emperor Akbar for religious discussions.

1600   Jesuits arrive in Lahore and build a church.

1601   Akbar allows his subjects to legally convert to Christianity.

1669   Mughal officials confiscate Carmelites' library.

1782–1799   Tipu Sultan's reign of terror.

1833   Protestant missionaries arrive to minister in northwestern India.

Circa 1860   Meg caste hears the gospel.

1860	Britain adds clause in Indian Penal Code making it a crime to offend the religion of another.
1873	Ditt converts and begins sharing the gospel with the Chuhras.
1906	Muslim League is formed.
1933	Students come up with the name "Pakistan."
1942	The "Quit India" campaign begins, inspired by Gandhi.
1947	Pakistan is founded, and Britain grants India independence.
1948	Mohammad al-Jinnah dies.
1949	Objectives Resolution is adopted.
1956	Pakistan's first constitution finalized.
1960	Esther John (formerly Qamar Zia) is martyred.
1962	Pakistan's constitution is revised and country renamed "the Republic of Pakistan."
1964	Pakistan's name amended back to "the Islamic Republic of Pakistan."
1973	President Bhutto adds provision in constitution that Islam is the state religion and the Prime Minister must be Muslim.

1977   General Zia Ul-Haq seizes power in a coup.

1978   Zia introduces Shariah benches.

1982   Amendment passes under Zia making it illegal to defile or destroy the Quran (Law 295b).

1986   Zia adds Law 295c, making it a crime to blaspheme Mohammed.

1991   Pakistan's first blasphemy case is filed against Gul Masih.

1997   Blasphemy accusations lead to the first mob attack on a village in Shanti Nagar.

2009   Muslims attack the villages of Korian and Gojra.

FOR FURTHER READING

The following books and websites were consulted in the writing of this book and are recommended for those interested in pursuing further study on the history of the persecuted church in Pakistan.

Anderson, William B. and Charles R. Watson. *Far North in India: A Survey of the Mission Field and Work of the United Presbyterian Church in the Punjab* (Philadelphia: The Board of Foreign Missions of the United Presbyterian Church of North America, 1911).

Bartolomeo, Fra. Paolino Da San. *A Voyage to the East Indies* (London: J. Davis, Chancery Lane, 1800).

Du Jarric, Pierre. *Akbar and the Jesuits* (New York: Harper & Brothers, 1926).

Gordon, Andrew. *Our India Mission: A Thirty Years' History of the India Mission of the United Presbyterian Church of North America* (Philadelphia: Andrew Gordon, 1888).

"Mr. Jinnah's presidential address to the Constituent Assembly of Pakistan" August 11, 1947. <www.pakistani.org/pakistan/legislation/constituent_address_11aug1947.html>. Accessed June 2, 2010.

Neill, Stephen. *The Story of the Christian Church in India and Pakistan* (Grand Rapids, MI: William B. Eerdmans Publishing Company, 1970).

Rooney, John. *The Hesitant Dawn: Christianity in Pakistan 1579–1760* (Rawalpindi: Christian Study Centre, 1984).

Rooney, John. *Shadows in the Dark: A History of Christianity in Pakistan Up to the 10th Century* (Rawalpindi: Christian Study Centre, 1984).

Sookhdeo, Patrick. *A People Betrayed: The Impact of Islamization on the Christian Community in Pakistan* (Ross-shire, Scotland: Christian Focus Publications, 2002).

Titus, Murray T. *Islam in India and Pakistan: A Religious History of Islam in India and Pakistan* (New Delhi: Munshiram Manoharlal Publishers, 2005).

Walbridge, Linda S. "The Christians of Pakistan: The Interaction of Law and Caste in Maintaining 'Outsider' Status," *Nationalism and Minority Identities in Islamic Societies*. Maya Shatzmiller, ed. (Montreal: McGill-Queen's University Press, 2005).

Webster, Warren. "Pakistan," *The Church in Asia*. Donald Hoke, ed. (Chicago: Moody Press, 1975).

Online Resources

The Voice of the Martyrs Websites:
    www.persecution.net (Canada)
    www.persecution.com (USA)

RESOURCES

The Voice of the Martyrs has many books, videos, brochures, and other products to help you learn more about the persecuted church. In the U.S., to order materials or receive our free monthly newsletter, call (800) 747-0085 or write to:

The Voice of the Martyrs
P.O. Box 443
Bartlesville, OK 74005-0443
www.persecution.com
thevoice@vom-usa.org

If you are in Australia, Canada, New Zealand, South Africa, or the United Kingdom, contact:

Australia:
Voice of the Martyrs
P.O. Box 250
Lawson NSW 2783
Australia

Website: www.persecution.com.au
Email: thevoice@persecution.com.au

Canada:
Voice of the Martyrs, Inc.
P.O. Box 608
Streetsville, ON L5M 2C1
Canada

Website: www.persecution.net
Email: thevoice@vomcanada.org

New Zealand:
> Voice of the Martyrs
> P.O. Box 5482
> Papanui, Christchurch 8542
> New Zealand
>
> Website: www.persecution.co.nz
> Email: thevoice@persecution.co.nz

South Africa:
> Christian Mission International
> P.O. Box 7157
> 1417 Primrose Hill
> South Africa
>
> Email: cmi@icon.co.za

United Kingdom:
> Release International
> P.O. Box 54
> Orpington BR5 9RT
> United Kingdom
>
> Website: www.releaseinternational.org
> Email: info@releaseinternational.org